Growing in Care
of the Earth

LIFE IN ABUNDANCE

◆ ◆ ◆ ◆ ◆

◆ ◆ ◆ ◆ ◆
LIFE IN ABUNDANCE

Growing in Care of the Earth

by
Virginia Pharr and Janet Watson

Saint Mary's Press
Christian Brothers Publications
Winona, Minnesota

Genuine recycled paper with 10% post-consumer waste.
Printed with soy-based ink.

The publishing team included Carl Koch, development editor; Laurie A. Berg, copy editor; James H. Gurley, production editor and typesetter; Maurine R. Twait, art director and cover designer; cover art, Don Bishop, Artville; pre-press, printing, and binding by the graphics division of Saint Mary's Press.

The acknowledgments continue on page 90.

Copyright © 1998 by Saint Mary's Press, 702 Terrace Heights, Winona, MN 55987-1320. All rights reserved. No part of this book may be reproduced by any means without the written permission of the publisher.

Printed in the United States of America

Printing: 9 8 7 6 5 4 3 2 1

Year: 2006 05 04 03 02 01 00 99 98

ISBN 0-88489-579-3

◆ ◆ ◆ ◆ ◆

In gratitude
    to my maternal grandmother
        Mamie Ray Hollander
    and to my mother
        Mary Hollander McCarthy
                  —*Virginia Pharr*

In gratitude
    to my mother
        Fern Lewis Watson
    and to my children
        Claire & Jude Watson Schreiner
                  —*Janet Watson*

Contents

Foreword   8
Introduction   16

The One Story   28
Cosmic Revival   30
Image of God   32
Knowing Earth   34
Wonder   36
Noticing   38
Gratefulness   40
Relationships   42
Divine Care   44
God as Mother-Father   46
Body of God   48
Galactic Visions   50
Creation as Healing   52
Prairie   54
Desert   56

♦ ♦ ♦ ♦ ♦

Seaside   *58*

Bears of the Forest   *60*

Insects   *62*

Trees   *64*

Gardening   *66*

Summer   *68*

Autumn   *70*

Circles   *72*

Darkness   *74*

Eating   *76*

Food   *78*

The Spirit of All Things   *80*

Time   *82*

Solitary Existence   *84*

Connection   *86*

Cosmic Dance   *88*

Foreword

Jesus said, . . . "I came that [you] may have life, and have it abundantly."

(John 10:7–10)

Jesus' mission is accomplished in each one of us when we nourish the seeds of full life that God has planted in the garden of our soul.

The following story suggests where the task of nurturing the seeds of abundant life needs to begin:

> "I was a revolutionary when I was young and all my prayer to God was 'Lord, give me the energy to change the world.'
>
> "As I approached middle age and realized that half my life was gone without my changing a single soul, I changed my prayer to 'Lord, give me the grace to change all those who come in contact with me. Just my family and friends, and I shall be satisfied.'
>
> "Now that I am an old man and my days are numbered, my one prayer is, 'Lord, give me the grace to change myself.' If I had prayed for this right from the start I should not have wasted my life."
>
> (Bayazid)

Jesus made this point much more saliently: "'Why do you see the speck in your neighbor's eye, but do not notice the log in your own eye? . . . Take the log out of your own eye, and then you will see clearly to take the speck out of your neighbor's eye'" (Matthew 7:3–5).

The meaning of Bayazid's story and Jesus' words is clear: we live life abundantly when we grow in the qualities of character that make life good. These qualities are traditionally called virtues—the inner readiness to do good.

Three Brilliant Flowers: Faith, Hope, Love

In the garden of the soul, faith, hope, and love form the centerpiece. They are essential for living abundantly, living fully. Traditionally called theological virtues, they come as free gifts from God and draw us to God. We cannot earn these qualities; God has already freely planted them in us.

Even so, faith, hope, and love need tending. In prayer, we can open our heart, mind, and will to God's grace. We embrace and open ourselves to this grace through reflection and conversation with God about what we believe, how we hope, and the ways we love. When we ponder the Scriptures and examine our beliefs, we nourish faith. When we meditate on the goodness of God's creation, on friendships, and on all God's gifts to us, we nourish hope. When we pray for loved ones, consider how we love, empathize with those needing love, and celebrate the love given to us, we nourish love. As faith, hope, and love spread and grow in the garden of our soul, we truly live life abundantly.

A Harvest of Plenty

The good life of faith, hope, and love is further nurtured as we develop the virtues of care of the earth, courage, justice, prudence, moderation, temperance, forgiveness, and so on. Saint Augustine and other spiritual teachers maintained that these virtues are expressions of faith, hope, and especially love. For instance, in the face of danger to a loved one, people find courage that they never dreamed they had. Living prudently—figuring out what is right in a given situation—becomes easier when love reigns in our heart and focuses our will.

Paradoxically, we find that as we grow in the moral virtues, we also nourish faith, hope, and love in ourselves.

For example, as we grow in justice, we begin to look out for the well-being of other people. In short, we grow more loving. Temperance—creating harmony within ourselves—fosters hopefulness.

Growing a Destiny

Growing abundant life means that we change ourselves by changing the small assertions of self, namely our acts, beginning with an act of prayer. The following wise adage provides a helpful way of thinking about how we can grow in abundance:

> Plant an act; reap a habit.
> Plant a habit; reap a virtue or vice.
> Plant a virtue or vice; reap a character.
> Plant a character; reap a destiny.

Developing our character and destiny begins with the acts that we plant each day, whether we do them consciously or unconsciously. We give shape to our life by each action we take, day by day. A regular pattern of actions becomes a habit. Eventually our habits determine the shape of our character.

Our character is the combination of our virtues and vices. Our destiny is what finally becomes of us, which depends on the character we build in response to God's grace. A Christlike destiny—life in abundance—begins forming with every act of moral virtue. When we pray to be caring of the earth, to be just, temperate, or moderate, when we pray for courage, honesty, and a forgiving spirit, we acknowledge our dependence on God's grace, but we also give our attention to the development of these qualities of character. Praying for moral virtue is planting, weeding, and watering virtuous acts. The harvest of such prayer will be life lived to the full.

We change the world by changing the small part of it that we are. An old adage says: "Prayer does not change things. Prayer changes people, and people change things." Prayer brings us to the God of love who wants us to have a good life, to live fully, to love, to believe, and to hope. If we open ourselves to God's grace, we will change. Then we can change things.

Praying for Life in Abundance

Virtue, like a garden, fails to thrive without attention and care. Prayer tends the garden. It also allows us to ask for forgiveness so that we can start again when we have left the garden untended. The loving God is always waiting to sustain us and to draw us back to full life. Our God is the God of Hosea who says about sinful and ungrateful Israel: "'I led them with cords of human kindness, with bands of love. I was to them like those who lift infants to their cheeks. I bent down to them and fed them'" (11:4).

Living abundantly leads us frequently to turn the care of the world over to God and to take care of our own soul. To deal with his tendency toward harshness, Vincent de Paul told one of his friends, "I turned to God and earnestly begged him to convert this irritable and forbidding trait of mine. I also asked for a kind and amiable spirit." Vincent's movement of heart toward God involved a surrender to God's presence and power. Vincent knew that living like Christ and clothing himself in Christ's virtues—living abundantly—had to begin with knowledge of his own sins and blessings. Times of prayer, the honest opening and offering of ourselves to God, provide the context for a change of heart, mind, and will to happen.

Praying for the virtues of full life may be roughly compared to tending a garden. "It was a great delight for me," writes Teresa of Ávila, "to consider my soul as a garden and reflect that the Lord was taking a walk in it." Prayer—the celebration of gratefulness for the goodness in life—invites God to walk in our garden. Prayer welcomes the Master Gardener to plant the seed of virtue within us. Prayer prepares the soil for the seed when it opens our fears, doubts, sins, and goodness to the gaze and grace of the Creator.

In the Epistle to the Ephesians, Paul tells the community to put on God's armor:

> Be strong in . . . the strength of [God's] power. . . . Take up the whole armor of God. . . . Fasten the belt of truth around your waist, and put on the breastplate of righteousness. As shoes for your feet put on whatever will make you ready to proclaim the gospel of peace. With all of these, take the shield of faith.
>
> (6:10–16)

To help us clothe ourselves in the armor of virtue necessary for a full life, the prayers in this book follow an ancient pattern: listen *(lectio),* reflect *(meditatio),* and respond *(oratio).* Here are some suggestions for using the prayers:

Listen. Each reflection begins with a passage from the word of God, the wisdom of a spiritual writer, or a story. Read the passage attentively at least once, or better yet, several times. Concentrate on one or two sentences that touch your heart; ponder their meaning for you and their effect on you. This type of listening is called *lectio divina,* or "divine studying." The passages are intended to inspire, challenge, or remind you of some essential aspect of the virtue.

Reflect. Once you have listened to wisdom, each meditation invites you to reflect on your own experience. This is *meditatio,* or "paying attention." Each reflection can help you attend to how God has been speaking to you in your past and present experience. If you keep a journal, you may want to write your reflections in it. Take the reflection questions with you as you go about your day; ponder them while you drive, wait for an appointment, prepare for bed, or find any moment of quiet.

Respond. Each reflection ends with a prayer of petition and thanks. In *oratio* we ask God for the help we need in nurturing the virtue that helps to form a good life. We should never be shy in asking God for help. After all, Jesus tells us many times to seek God's grace, and he assures us that God's help will come. Indeed, the word *prayer* means "to obtain by entreaty." The petitionary prayer reminds us that we are truly dependent on the goodness and love of God for developing the virtue. The response prayer usually gives thanks for the gifts God has showered upon us already. Giving thanks is another way of waking us up to all the wonders of God's love.

Try reading the prayers aloud. They gain a different feel and power. Or use one line as a prayer throughout the day. Plant the prayer line in your heart as you repeat it while having a cup of coffee, washing your hands, or sitting at your desk.

Starting Points

Create a sacred space. Jesus said, "'When you pray, go to your private room, shut yourself in, and so pray to your [God] who is in that secret place, and your [God] who sees all that is done in secret will reward you'" (Matthew 6:6). Solitary prayer is best done in a place where you can have privacy and silence, both of which can be luxuries in the life of a busy person. If privacy and silence are not possible, create a quiet, safe place within yourself, perhaps while riding to and from work, sitting at the dentist's office, or waiting for someone. Do the best you can, knowing that a loving God is present everywhere.

Move into sacred time. All of time is suffused with God's presence. So remind yourself that God is present as you begin your prayer. If something keeps intruding during your prayer, spend some time talking with God about it. Be flexible, because God's Spirit blows where it will. Gerald May speaks to this when he says:

> The present . . . contains everything that is needed for lovingly beginning the next moment; it seeks only our own willing, responsive presence, just here, just now. . . . There are not exceptions—not in physical pain, not in psychiatric disorder or emotional agony, not in relational strife. . . . Love is too much with us for there to be any exceptions.

Come to prayer with an open mind, heart, and will. Trust that God hears you and wants to support your desire to nourish the virtues of a good life. Prayer can strengthen our will to act. Through prayer God can touch our will and empower us to live according to what we know is true.

Prayer is essential to creating life in abundance because it nourishes the seeds of virtue that are planted in our soul. Listening to wisdom fertilizes the seed. Reflecting on or attending to the virtue waters the seed. Responding with petitionary and thanksgiving prayers shines light on the seed. After reflecting and praying about care of the earth, you will have planted the seed in rich soil so that it can grow. As it grows it will become a bright flower in the garden of your soul.

God be with you as you grow in care of the earth and in living life to the full. You will be a power for the good of us all.

CARL KOCH
Editor

Introduction

The Earth Story

We are a storied people. Our sacred texts are filled with stories of faith, longing, liberation from a land of oppression, liberation to a land of promise and life in abundance. Stories can free and transform us. A well-crafted story has the power to change hearts and move people to action. At this turn of the millennium, an ancient story is being told—the story of Creation and how we might renew our place within its sacred telling, "In the beginning . . . God created the heavens and the earth" (Genesis 1:1).

Growing in care of the earth starts by entering into the story of all creation. So, welcome to a story of origins and beginnings. Welcome to a story of care. Welcome to a story regarding nothing more than the simplicity of a garden and nothing less than planetary survival. The story of this earth garden is vast and complex. Its roots reach deep into the soil of communal faith. Its boughs stretch out against a horizon of global issues. Essentially, this story is about whether or not we, the human ones, will learn to live with the other creatures who share our garden home. Will life be abundant for all the inhabitants, for only a few of them, or for none of them?

Telling creation's story requires legions of voices and a great capacity for listening. It requires patience to hear what a stone, an ocean, a companion animal, or another woman or man is saying. Telling the story requires a heart turned with deference toward other perspectives, realizing that a human viewpoint is simply one of many. It requires the stark honesty to admit that living from a *human only-human first* attitude has imperiled the other creatures who share our garden home and the planet itself.

God said, "Let us make humankind in our image, according to our likeness; and let them have dominion over the fish of the sea, and over the birds of the air, and over the cattle, and over all the wild animals of the earth, and over every creeping thing that creeps upon the earth."

. . . God said, "See, I have given you every plant yielding seed that is upon the face of all the earth, and every tree with seed in its fruit; you shall have them for food. And to every beast of the earth, and to every bird of the air, and to everything that creeps on the earth, everything that has the breath of life, I have given every green plant for food." And it was so. God saw everything, . . . and indeed, it was very good.

(Genesis 1:26–31)

Every religious myth derives from this larger, older story of Creation. Through experiencing life in relationship to plants, animals, and the elements, our ancestors in faith dared to reflect on their beginnings. Surely the earth, so plentiful and generous in providing sustenance, had been given to humanity by a loving God.

In the past several decades, our religious stories regarding the genesis of earth and humanity have been complemented by a new story of creation. The new story simply affirms that through the love of the Creator, over fifteen billion years ago, the universe burst into existence. Earth was born from the dust of exploding stars over four-and-one-half billion years ago. All the gases and elements that coalesced and cooled over the following years formed intricate patterns, colors, shapes, and, eventually, life itself. We humans, according to this new story, are the first creatures on the planet who are able to reflect on our four and one-half-billion-year genesis. We are the first to consciously affirm and echo the words of God, "It [is] very good."

Our ancestors in faith, so moved by their experience of exile and their hopes of liberation, wove a creation story that imagined all things had been created by God for them. Humans were to be the masters of creation. The new story affirms that humans have a special role in creation, but that we also are dependent upon the planet and all creatures. Humans, then, are to be masters, but masters of care.

A master is a person who has become skilled, proficient, and qualified in a particular area. In the new story, humans are masters of two things: reflective thinking and the ability to care. We are created to be thoughtful and caring toward our planet and all its inhabitants. Both our tradition and the new story bear this out.

The Body of God

The Christian Scriptures are filled with references to the importance of bodies. Jesus touched, healed, fed, and raised bodies. Again and again the Scriptures portray Jesus as caring for bodies. In the account of the healing of Jairus's daughter, Jesus brings life amid the disbelief of his critics. Jesus says to them:

> "The child is not dead but sleeping." And they laughed at him. Then he put them all outside, and took the child's father and mother and those who were with him, and went in where the child was. He took her by the hand and said to her, "Talitha cum," which means, "Little girl, get up!" And immediately the girl got up and began to walk about. . . . At this they were overcome with amazement.
>
> (Mark 5:39–42)

Like the little girl in this Scripture story, we humans could be said to have been sleeping. The new story—our new comprehension of our role on earth—calls us to wake up to our proper place in the scheme of God's creation.

As the community of faith that carries on the work of Christ in the world, we are called to care for all the bodies on the planet. One way to do this is to read the Scriptures with ecological eyes, imagining that the peregrine falcon, the humpback whale, and the rain forests are the bodies being touched by Christ through our hands today.

A vibrant faith in the God of creation lets us see that Paul's analogy of the body can be extended to the natural order.

> God arranged the members in the body, each one of them. . . . If all were a single member, where would the body be? As it is, there are many members, yet one body. The eye cannot say to the hand, "I have no need of you," nor again the head to the feet, "I have no need of you." On the contrary, the members of the body that seem to be weaker are indispensable, and those members of the body that we think less honorable we clothe with greater honor.
>
> (1 Corinthians 12:18–23)

Our role is to care intensely for the least of our brothers and sisters on the planet. Trees would fare quite splendidly without human intervention. But it is we who depend on the life cycle of trees to create an oxygen-rich atmosphere for us.

Sallie McFague asks, "What if we dared to think of our planet and indeed the entire universe as the body of God?" Cousin to the stars, brother and sister to earth's creatures, we humans are challenged by the new story to redefine ourselves in the scope of God's creation. Given this understanding, Paul could just as easily have said:

We are all one body, though many parts. A human cannot say to the air, "I have no need of you." Nor can the air say to the tree, "I have no need of you." On the contrary, every part of creation is indispensable if we are to have life in abundance.

With this understanding of our interdependence with all creation, we may daily celebrate the Incarnation—God's bodiliness among us—in a richer, fuller way. We are beginning to comprehend that God's spirit moves within all things. All creatures participate in God's body. All creation gives forth the God-light out of which it is created.

Just as we are called to liberation in Christ, the whole creation is eagerly awaiting the revelation of God's sons and daughters. It is not from any fault on the part of creation that it was made unable to attain its purpose:

> Creation waits with eager longing for the revealing of the children of God; for the creation was subjected to futility . . . in hope that the creation itself will be set free from its bondage to decay and will obtain the freedom of the glory of the children of God. We know that the whole creation has been groaning in labor pains until now.
>
> (Romans 8:19–22)

Through us, the earth waits, longs. Through birds, the earth flies. Through trees, the earth breathes. Through oceans, the earth roars. Through cats, the earth purrs. And God is glorified. But always, earth waits for us to care for it as a member of Christ's body, as a beloved part of ourselves.

At Home in God's House

The word *ecology* has come to mean many things, but its origin manifests its essence. It comes from two Greek words: *eco* from *oikos,* meaning "household," and *logy* from *logos,* meaning "word" or "expression." The poet D. H. Lawrence expresses the nature of ecology this way:

> All that matters is to be at one with the living God
> to be a creature in the house of the God of Life.
>
> Like a cat asleep on a chair
> at peace, in peace
>
> and at one with the master of the house, with the mistress,
> at home, at home in the house of the living,
> sleeping on the hearth, and yawning before the fire.
>
> Sleeping on the hearth of the living world,
> yawning at home before the fire of life
> feeling the presence of the living God
> like a great reassurance
> a deep calm in the heart.

So, ecology is about learning the guidelines of behavior (*ethos*) for the household (*oikos*). The earth is our home, and in order for us to experience the deep peace of "yawning at home before the fire of life," we need to learn the boundaries, guidelines, and behaviors that will make peace possible. Ultimately, care involves learning the boundaries, words, and expressions of another person or creature and respecting them as well as we do our own. At its heart, ecology is caring for the earth. We grow in care of the earth by each act of gratitude, each act of respect, each act of tending that we do for creation.

Certainly, ecology and justice go hand in hand. It is impossible to feel at home where there is oppression.

Oftentimes, when we feel the effects of pollution, overconsumption, and human wastefulness, we long, as did our enslaved Hebrew ancestors in faith, for another land, another home where justice for all God's creatures is possible. But the new story tells us clearly that we have no other land save our own. We now realize that the earth is a onetime endowment. The basic question the earth asks is, "Shall we humans honor the four and one-half billion years it took to create our home, or shall we continue to live beyond its limits?" Or, as Simone Weil asks, "How can Christianity call itself catholic if the universe itself is left out?"

We humans need only look to the beauty and order of earth systems to learn how to live within limits. Simone Weil says, "The beauty of the world is Christ's tender smile coming to us through matter. [Christ] is really present in the universal beauty." We will learn how to care for the planet and other creatures, including human ones, by observing and appreciating the earth in its cycles and seasons.

Starting with a Garden

We are all gardeners of the earth. Everything we do either tends the garden or harms it. If we wish to learn care of the earth, a good place to start is in a garden.

Time spent caringly in a garden returns us to the story and to the soil. It introduces us to our "ecological self" and teaches us to live at home on earth. In the garden we learn from the soil, plants, and elements how to form community and honor the rhythm and cycles of life in that community. We learn to let ourselves be vulnerable to creation, to allow our beliefs and our faith to be crafted by an intimate relationship with the planet in a particular place.

The act of gardening, for Jesus, was a rich metaphor. It provided a way to speak to his hearers about the importance of God's word. Jesus lived close to the land, as his stories and parables show.

> "Listen! A sower went out to sow. And as he sowed, some seed fell on the path, and the birds came and ate it up. Other seed fell on rocky ground, where it did not have much soil, and it sprang up quickly, since it had no depth of soil. And when the sun rose, it was scorched; and since it had no root, it withered away. . . . Other seed fell into good soil and brought forth grain, growing up and increasing and yielding thirty and sixty and a hundredfold."
> (Mark 4:3–8)

Jesus' listeners understood the importance of God's word because they first understood the importance of successful planting. They understood that life in abundance, planting God's word in our soul, and being good gardeners to the earth are all entwined.

Indeed, gardeners gradually learn about the particularities of their garden. This soil, these invader species, that weather pattern—all serve to reveal something about how to care concretely for the planet. In the same way that no two people are exactly alike, no two gardens and no two creatures are the same. Caring includes observing and respecting differences.

Life in a garden community requires something of the gardeners: it requires coming home to their senses. In the act of gardening, of turning the soil and tenderly encouraging their plantings, gardeners are led to see, touch, taste, feel, hear, and intuit in a new way. They also develop another sense, a sense of place. Gardeners begin to experience the garden as unique, sacred, holy ground.

The earth is our garden home where God plants and tends. Perhaps gardeners especially will gradually become aware of this. Those who garden will sooner or later come to ponder the subtle truth: "I am the gardener. I am the gardened." This is particularly true at harvest time, when the garden invites others into the sense of place the gardener has developed. Those who share the fruits of the garden are drawn into a communion with the garden space. All who eat what the garden produces are being nourished by the gifts of a particular place.

*C*elebrating Places

Geography forms spirituality. We need to have a sense of place if we are to have a rich inner life, if we are to be filled with the desire "to do justice, and to love kindness, and to walk humbly with [our] God" (Micah 6:8), if we are to care for the earth. Each geographical place is a unique bioregion, where life rules in different, particular ways. The desert is not the Great Plains, is not the seaside, is not the mountains. To be in the community of life in a particular geographical region teaches us different things.

> Why do we have such a wonderful idea of God? Because we live in such a gorgeous world. We wonder at the magnificence of whatever it is that brought the world into being. This leads to a sense of adoration. We have a sense of immense gratitude that we participate in such a beautiful world. This adoration, this gratitude, we call religion. Now, however, as the outer world is diminished, our inner world is dried up.
> . . . Imagination is required for religious development. What would there be to imagine if we lived on the moon? We would have something, but it would be very meagre. Our sensitivities would be

dull because our inner world would reflect the outer world.

(Thomas Berry)

As we experience our landscape, our sense of place, so we experience the divine.

Our ancestors in faith knew the spiritual power of place. Mountains were celebrated as meeting places with Yahweh.

> Who has the right to climb Yahweh's mountain?
> Or stand in this holy place?
> Those who are pure in act and in thought.
>
> (Psalm 24:3–4)

Psalm 104 celebrates place by extolling God for creating such diversity.

> Bless Yahweh, O my soul.
> How great you are, Yahweh, my God!
> You are clothed in majesty and splendor,
> wrapped in a robe of light!
> You spread the heavens out like a tent;
> you build your high walls upon the waters above.
> The clouds are your chariot
> as you travel on the wings of the wind.
> The breezes are your messengers
> and fiery flames your servants.
> . . . .
> You set springs gushing in ravines,
> flowing between the mountains,
> giving drink to wild animals,
> drawing the thirsty wild donkeys.
> The birds of the air make their nests
> and sing among the branches nearby.
> . . . .

> The trees of Yahweh are well watered—
> those cedars of Lebanon.
> Here the birds build their nest;
> and, on the highest branches, the stork has its
> > home.
> For the wild goats there are the mountains;
> badgers hide in the rocks.
>
> (Psalm 104:1–4,10–18)

The psalmist recognizes and celebrates that God has created a welcoming world where all creatures should be able to live in abundance and find a home.

The Creator invites us to celebrate place through song, poetry, and our senses, but also by appreciating, tending, protecting, and cleansing. In celebrating place, we celebrate the Creator. After all, all places are "'holy ground'" (Exodus 3:5) because God abides in all places.

Sharing Hospitality

Jesus lived in a culture where hospitality was essential. Sharing food was part of that hospitality. Jesus fed the multitudes, identified himself with bread and wine, and cooked fish over the charcoal fire for his friends after the Resurrection. Eating, in our spiritual tradition, has profound meaning.

The ethos of our household—ecology—invites us to consider eating together in a new light: as communion. We are invited to see God's body in every meal we share. Sacramental Communion takes on special significance as we become sensitive and attuned to sharing God's body. When we are aware that the food on our plate, as well as those who prepare it, has sacrificed on our behalf, we become more deeply immersed in the meaning of Jesus as the Bread of Life. We become more aware of our oneness, our communion with the created order.

When we share the goods of creation, especially food, with one another with the same hospitality that Jesus urged, we grow in our care of the earth. We realize in new and poignant ways what love of God and neighbor is all about. Do we thank God for the food we share? Do we savor mindfully the fruits of creation? Do we linger at table with one another? Do we spend as much time feasting on a homecooked meal as we do preparing it? Care of the earth can be learned in every bite and in the communion of spirit at every table.

Growing in Care of the Earth

Creation, like the bread of hospitality offered by our ancestors of faith, is a gift. As we welcome another creature, we welcome a part of ourselves. When we care for any body in creation, we care for ourselves, too. We are so intimately connected that whatever happens to any member of the body happens to the whole body.

The world in all its diversity and life forms is a gift from the Creator. Care for creation is the action of a grateful heart. When we meditate and pray to grow in care of the earth, when we take care of Brother Wind, Sister Water, Mother Earth, as Francis of Assisi calls them, we build the Reign of God. Then:

> The wilderness and the dry land shall be glad,
> > the desert shall rejoice and blossom;
> like the crocus it shall blossom abundantly,
> > and rejoice with joy and singing.
> . . . .
> They shall see the glory . . .
> > the majesty of our God.
>
> (Isaiah 35:1–2)

Then all creation will live life in abundance.

The One Story

Listen

There is eventually only one story, the story of the universe. Every form of being is integral with this comprehensive story. Nothing is itself without everything else. Each member of the Earth community has its own proper role within the entire sequence of transformations that have given shape and identity to everything that exists.

(Brian Swimme and Thomas Berry)

❖ ❖ ❖ ❖ ❖

Reflect

The universe story offers two central themes for our consideration: privilege and responsibility. The privilege of membership in the earth community assures us that we need never be alone. The responsibility of engaging in meaningful and transformative work on behalf of the entire community is part of our proper role within the sequence.

 Reflect on your membership in the earth community by bringing to awareness the other members of this vast community. Recall members of the earth community with whom you have interacted in the last few moments. How do you express your responsibility to the earth community?

Respond

I thank you, Creator of the universe, for the privilege of being a part of this wonderful design. Give me the insight and conviction to carry out my responsibilities as part of this earth community. Help me do my part to bring about the transformation that is essential to the ongoing creation story.

Cosmic Revival

Listen

The world is almost unimaginably *old*: about 15 billion years ago a single numinous speck exploded in an outpouring of matter and energy, shaping a universe that is still expanding. Five billion years ago an aging, first generation star exploded, spewing out elements that coalesced to form our sun and its planets, including Earth. *The human is only recently arrived.*

The world is almost incomprehensibly *large*: over one hundred billion galaxies, each comprised of one hundred billion stars, and no one knows how many moons and planets, all of this visible and audible matter being only a fraction of the matter in the universe. *We humans inhabit a small planet orbiting a medium-sized star toward the edge of one spiral galaxy.*

The world is almost mind-numbingly *dynamic*: out of the Big Bang, the stars; out of the stardust, the Earth; out of the Earth, single-celled living creatures; out of evolutionary life and death of these creatures, human beings with a consciousness and freedom that concentrates the self-transcendence of matter itself. *Human beings are the universe become conscious of itself. We are the cantors of the universe.*

(Elizabeth Johnson)

Reflect

Humility and pride seem to be appropriate responses to our place in a universe so old, so large, so dynamic. The more we learn about the universe, the less significant we may seem. Yet, we are here for however long, struggling to imagine, to comprehend, and to echo a canticle of response to the awesomeness of it all. Wonder is the beginning of philosophy, so say the ancients. Wonder is also a fitting response to the earth, and it certainly stirs us to care for the earth.

Close your eyes, relax, breathe deeply, and then imagine that you are out in space—as the astronauts have been—looking back at the earth. How does that make you feel? Now, eyes closed, imagine a cell in your body—one, single cell. How does that make you feel? Finally, imagine a single atom in that cell. Talk to the Creator about all this.

Respond

Sing out your joy to the Creator, good people;
for praise is fitting for loyal hearts.
Give thanks to the Creator upon the harp,
with a ten-stringed lute sing songs.
O sing a new song;
play skillfully and loudly so all may hear.
For the word of the Creator is faithful,
and all God's works are to be trusted.

(Psalm 33:1–4)

Image of God

Listen

In this community of all creation each species has its own unique place. Every creature bears the "stamp of origin" of the creator, the one primordial ground of all being. Every type of creature, then, must be understood as reflecting something of the mystery of the creator. Humankind is part of a world of beings which are all related to one another as one community grounded in the life of God.

(Denis Edwards)

◆ ◆ ◆ ◆ ◆

Reflect

Denis Edwards invites us to expand our understanding of who and what reflect the mystery of the Creator of our world. Humankind is one of the magnificent reflections of the Creator. Countless others add to the mystery.

Recall when you have been aware of the reflection of the mystery of the Creator in another species. If you need a starting point, look out your window, take a trip around the block, pick up your dog or cat. Offer a prayer of thanksgiving for that member or those members of the cosmic family.

Respond

I am honored, holy Creator, to bear your "stamp of origin." I ask for the wisdom to know how I am to reflect your mystery to the world in a way that respects all the rest of your beloved creation.

Knowing Earth

Listen

For it is [wisdom] who gave me unerring knowledge of
    what exists,
to know the structure of the world and the activity of the
    elements;
the beginning and end and middle of times,
the alternations of the solstices and the changes of the
    seasons,
the cycles of the year and the constellations of the stars,
the natures of animals and the tempers of wild animals,
the powers of spirits and the thoughts of human beings,
the varieties of plants and the virtues of roots;
I learned both what is secret and what is manifest,
for wisdom, the fashioner of all things, taught me.
                    (Wisdom of Solomon 7:17–22)

◆ ◆ ◆ ◆ ◆

Reflect

This passage from the Book of the Wisdom of Solomon illustrates the importance of carefully observing the universe and being patiently open to the lessons it has to teach. This sound knowledge is not for the scientist alone. Wisdom reveals hidden mysteries to those with the love, the desire, and the heart to pursue them. So often the wisdom of God manifests itself through our experiences in nature: walking outdoors, sitting on a beach, weeding a garden. So near, yet, at times, unnoticed. Make a resolution to be more observant of aspects of creation closest to home.

If you can, go outside somewhere, sit quietly or walk softly, and absorb the sounds all around you. Offer the Creator a response, and talk to the Creator about other ways of knowing the earth.

Respond

Holy wisdom of God, grant me the patience and perseverance to be open to the lessons the natural world has to teach me. Gift me with the love, desire, and heart to pursue the hidden mysteries nature holds in store for me.

Wonder

Listen

Wonder may well be what is special about us from the perspective of the common creation story. One of the most profound lessons we can learn from the common creation story is appreciation for life, not just our own, but that of all the other creatures in the family of life. We are the ones, the only ones on our planet, who know the story of life and the only ones who know that we know: the only ones capable of being filled with wonder, surprise, curiosity, and fascination by it.

(Sallie McFague)

◆ ◆ ◆ ◆ ◆

Reflect

When one thinks of wonder, children naturally come to mind. We use the phrase "childlike wonder" to describe innocent observation, seeing things as though for the first time. In their own world, children become pure acts of attention to the simplest and the most complex things around them. The creation story invites us to recover the wonder, surprise, curiosity, and fascination that was our birthright as children.

Reflect on the state of wonder in your life. Observe a child watching the natural world. Allow creation to become a source of wonder to you again, perhaps by focusing your attention on one of its wonders: a leaf, an orange, a goldfish, a glass of milk, a stone. Feel it, smell it, listen to it—be present. Give thanks.

Respond

There are days, O God, when wonder, surprise, curiosity, and fascination are simply fond memories. I miss that part of myself. Help me rekindle the flames of wonder in my mind and heart, so that I may appreciate your gifts more fully.

Noticing

Listen

But one day when I was sitting quiet and feeling like a motherless child, which I was, it come to me: that feeling of being part of everything, not separate at all. I knew that if I cut a tree, my arm would bleed. And I laughed and I cried and I run all around the house. . . .

God love everything you love—and a mess of stuff you don't. But more than anything else God love admiration.

You saying God vain? I ast.

Naw, she say. Not vain, just wanting to share a good thing. I think it pisses God off if you walk by the color purple in a field somewhere and don't notice it.

What it do when it pissed off? I ast.

Oh, it make something else. People think pleasing God is all God care about. But any fool living in the world can see it always trying to please us back.

Yeah? I say.

Yeah, she say. It always making little surprises and springing them on us when us least expect.

You mean it want to be loved, just like the bible say.

Yes, Celie, she say. Everything want to be loved.

(Alice Walker)

◆ ◆ ◆ ◆ ◆

Reflect

What a refreshing insight! More than anything else, God loves admiration. Much of our life we are instructed in the adoration of a distant God. We adore God; we do not adore creation. Is it possible that we adore God without admiring God?

When did you last experience admiration for God as you walked by "the color of purple in a field somewhere"? Consider the distinction between "adoration" and "admiration." Ponder the last couple of hours, and ask yourself, Was there a time during the day when God was "trying to please us back"? Offer a prayer of admiration.

Respond

Forgive me, Divine Artist, for all the times I failed to notice the color purple, or any other color for that matter. Forgive me for the times I adored you without admiring you and your work. I promise to be more attentive and appreciative from now on. Alleluia!

Gratefulness

Listen

The gift within every gift is always opportunity. Most of the time, it is the opportunity to rejoice and to delight in the moment. Not often enough do we pay attention to the many opportunities we have each day simply to enjoy: the sun shining through the trees, dew glistening on a just-opened flower, the smile of a baby, the embrace of a friend. We can sleepwalk through life until something comes that we cannot enjoy; only then are we startled awake. If we were to learn to avail ourselves of those countless opportunities to enjoy, to dwell in the gift of being alive, then, when the moment comes to do something difficult, we could see that, too, as an opportunity and gratefully take advantage of it.

Life is given to us; every moment is given. The only appropriate response therefore is gratefulness. When we wake up to the fact that everything is a gift, it is only natural to be thankful and to look on everything that happens as a chance to respond to the Given Life.

(David Steindl-Rast)

❖ ❖ ❖ ❖ ❖

Reflect

Almost without our knowing it, our life becomes complex, fast-paced. To use efficiency terms, we engage in multitasking, polyphasic activity. We do several things simultaneously. None receive our undivided attention. We say to ourselves that we are going to slow down, take time to smell the roses.

None of us is alone in this desire for simplicity. Spiritual books abound on the simple life, the back-to-nature lifestyle. We long to focus on and appreciate one thing at a time.

Find a favorite food. If you have oranges, they are ideal for this gratefulness activity. Go off by yourself with your orange or some other food. Take a full 15 minutes to eat whatever it is. Take your time to relish the feel, smell, and taste as you peel or unwrap it. Take small bites, roll it around on your tongue, chew and swallow slowly, deliberately. If you get distracted, remind yourself, "I'm eating this orange." Resolve to focus on, and appreciate, one thing of beauty today, two things tomorrow, three things the next day. Gift yourself with the chance to respond to the "Given Life" with mindful gratefulness.

Respond

I am sick and tired of sleepwalking through life, O God. My life gets so hectic that I rarely notice opportunities for what they are: invitations from you to embrace the moment. Grace me, please, with a new sense of delight. Help me to recognize opportunities to grow.

Relationships

Listen

Nothing exists outside relationships. Ecology reaffirms the interdependence of beings, interprets all hierarchies as a matter of function, and repudiates the so-called right of the strongest. . . . All being constitutes a link in the vast cosmic chain. As Christians, we may say that it comes from God and returns to God.

(Leonardo Boff)

Respond

Careful observation of the natural world reveals how wonderfully interconnected it all is. Sometimes we forget that we, too, are "a link in the vast cosmic chain," though not the strongest, or the most important. We can imagine that this cosmos, our planet, can exist—even thrive—without humankind. Humans cannot survive without our planet.

Meditate on your place in the vast cosmic chain. Visualize yourself as a part of, rather than apart from, all the rest of creation. Pondering the day, what interdependencies are immediately life-giving?

Reflect

For my link in the cosmic chain of life, I am ever grateful, Creator God. I have faith that creation comes from you and returns to you. May my time in between be a time of cocreating with you for the betterment of all creation.

Divine Care

Listen

All creatures depend on you
to give them food in due season.
You give the food they eat;
with generous hand, you fill them with good things.
If you turn your face away—they suffer;
if you stop their breath—they die and return to dust.
When you give your spirit, they are created.
You keep renewing the world.

(Psalm 104:27–30)

Reflect

This psalmist sings a song of praise and faith describing the people's understanding and experience of God's relationship to them and to their daily needs. As part of the Covenant, Yahweh has responsibilities to the community. It is not a one-sided agreement. This brings to mind the character Tevya in *Fiddler on the Roof*. Throughout the play, Tevya's heartfelt dialogs with God indicate his unwillingness to let God off the hook. Tevya keeps his part of the bargain as best he knows how, and he invites God to do the same.

Ask yourself: What are my expectations of how and what God will provide? Have I let God off the hook? Invite God into a covenant relationship again.

Respond

It is comforting, God of the Covenant, that you promise to be a partner in the process of caring for the earth. You promise to provide for your faithful people. I ask you to keep that promise and to give us concrete signs that we can hold on to in good times and in bad times. Do not forget that we are in this together.

*G*od as Mother-Father

*L*isten

God is not only the Father of all good things, but . . . the mother of all things as well. [God] is Father, . . . the cause of all things and their creator. [God] is the mother, for when creatures have received their being . . . [God] still stays with them to keep them in being. If God did not remain with . . . creatures after they had started their own life, they would quickly fall out of being.

(Meister Eckhart)

♦ ♦ ♦ ♦ ♦

Reflect

Many people look to the Native American tradition for rich familial creation imagery. Mother Earth, Father Sky come to mind. The Judeo-Christian tradition is replete with parental images of a creating God. Jesus used both paternal and maternal images when referring to God as, for example, "a hen gather[ing] her brood under her wings" (Luke 13:34). Meister Eckhart understood the importance of connecting the paternal and maternal aspects of God's relationship to all created things.

Close your eyes. Imagine how our Mother-Father God cares for the earth. What gives you assurance that God remains with all creatures?

Respond

I look to you, Mother-Father God, for the nurturance all life needs to survive and thrive. Without your loving care and concern, I feel disconnected from the source of my being and from all other beings. Strengthen my relationship with you and with all creation.

Body of God

Listen

The body of God is not a body, but all the different, peculiar, particular bodies about us. . . . We do not use nature or other people as a means to an end—our union with God—but see each and every creature, every body, as intrinsically valuable in itself, in its specialness, its distinctiveness, its difference from ourselves. . . . The model of the world as God's body encourages us to dare to love bodies and find them valuable and wonderful—just that and nothing more. The "God part" will take care of itself if we can love and value the bodies.

(Sallie McFague)

❖ ❖ ❖ ❖ ❖

Reflect

Gospel stories about the historical Jesus reveal him to be a consummate healer of bodies. In fact, Jesus was considered by many to be blasphemous because he unlawfully healed on the Sabbath (Mark 3:1–6). He considered the healthy body to be as important as the Sabbath.

Sallie McFague offers a fresh God-image for our consideration—the entire world as God's body; all bodies, God's body. In the film *Litany of the Great River*, the artist Meinrad Craighead speaks of the sum total of all the heartbeats in the universe as God's own heartbeat—the world as God's body; all heartbeats, God's heartbeat.

Reread Mark 3:1–6. Pause and reflect: Would you treat your body and the body of the world differently if you believed them to be the very body of God? Resolve to add this image of God to your understanding of the relationship between God and creation.

Respond

The world as your body! This is a new image for me, God of the universe, and it is going to take some getting used to. But I like it. The world as your body—I am excited by how much better we might care for the world if we know we are caring for you. The body of God, the body of God.

Galactic Visions

Listen

Tonight on every continent humans will look into the edge of the Milky Way, that band of stars our ancestors compared to a road, a pathway to heaven, a flowing river of milk. . . .

Humans tonight will watch the Milky Way galaxy not only with eyes, but also with radio telescopes, satellites, and computer-guided optical telescopes, with minds trained by the intricate theories of the composition, structure, and dynamic evolution of matter. Though we wait as faithfully as the ancient Inuit who stared eye-to-eye with a blue-black whale, we will not see a galactic eye blinking back at us. Though we may be as dedicated to the wild spirit of the night sky, no eye of the universe will appear from behind a cloud. . . . For after such long centuries of inquiry, we find that the universe developed over fifteen billion years, and that the eye that searches the Milky Way galaxy is itself an eye shaped by the Milky Way. The mind that searches for contact with the Milky Way is the very mind of the Milky Way galaxy in search of its inner depths.

(Brian Swimme and Thomas Berry)

◆ ◆ ◆ ◆ ◆

Reflect

For endless ages human beings have had a love affair with the heavens. We eagerly await the darkness to be able to see more clearly what is not so readily apparent in the light of day. We gaze endlessly at the stars and planets. They are our inspiration in times of love, our guide in times of longing and exploration. The Hubble telescope has brought the awesome vastness of it all closer than ever before. Yet, sometimes, on a very dark night, we find ourselves reaching out to touch the nearest star.

The heavens declare the glory of God. Choose a clear, dark night. Go outside. Stand under the starlit sky, and gaze into the heavens. Keep vigil. Watch the heavens declare God's glory. Offer a spontaneous response.

Respond

The heavens proclaim your glory, O God,
and the firmament shows forth
the work of your hands.
Day carries the news to day
and night brings the message to night.
No speech, no word,
no voice is heard;
yet their news goes forth through all the earth,
their words to the farthest bounds of the world.
(Psalm 19:1–4)

Creation as Healing

Listen

The reasons for depression are not so interesting as the way one handles it, simply to stay alive. This morning I woke at four and lay awake for an hour or so in a bad state. It is raining again. I got up finally and went about the daily chores, waiting for the sense of doom to lift—and what did it was watering the house plants. Suddenly joy came back because I was fulfilling a simple need, a living one. Dusting never has this effect (and that may be why I am such a poor housekeeper!), but feeding the cats when they are hungry, giving Punch clean water, makes me suddenly feel calm and happy.

Whatever peace I know rests in the natural world, in feeling myself a part of it, even in a small way. Maybe the gaiety of the Warner family, their wisdom, comes from this, that they work close to nature all the time. As simple as that? But it is not simple. Their life requires patient understanding, imagination, the power to endure constant adversity—the weather, for example! To go with, not against the elements.

(May Sarton)

Reflect

May Sarton expresses clearly what many of us know from firsthand experience: that the natural world is a faithful healer of the body, mind, and spirit. For many people today, peace is found in outdoor activity—jogging, walking, gardening, bird feeding, bird-watching. Indoor gardening, cooking with herbs, or caring for our four-legged family members can bring a powerful sense of well-being during trying times and times of tranquillity. Our health and well-being benefit from feeling that we are part of the natural world.

Examine and inventory the ways in which you feel yourself connected to the natural world. What are the benefits you derive from the connection? If you have lost the connection, recover at least one way you can become reconnected.

Respond

Healing God, I am so very grateful for the parts of your creation that rely on my care. Ironically, in caring for and connecting with them, I find relief, or maybe distraction, from my own physical and emotional pain. Maybe it's because I don't feel so isolated from the rest of the natural world. I have learned that not just humans bear one another's burdens. Thank you for your healing creation.

Prairie

Listen

The so-called emptiness of the Plains is full of such miraculous "little things." The way native grasses spring back from a drought, greening before your eyes; the way a snowy owl sits on a fencepost, or a golden eagle hunts, wings outstretched over grassland that seems to go on forever. Pelicans rise noisily from a lake; an antelope stands stock-still, its tattooed neck like a message in unbreakable code; columbines, their long stems beaten down by hail, bloom in the mud, their whimsical and delicate flowers intact. One might see a herd of white-tailed deer jumping a fence; fox cubs wrestling at the door of their lair; cock pheasants stepping out of a medieval tapestry into windrowed hay; cattle bunched in the southeast corner of a pasture, anticipating a storm in the approaching thunderheads. And above all, one notices the quiet, the near-absence of human noise.

(Kathleen Norris)

Reflect

Every religious tradition values the potentially sacred time of human silence. Whether it is called silent prayer, meditation, contemplation, or a silent retreat, one purpose of the silence is to make listening possible—to hear what the rest of creation has to say to us, to make us aware that the human voice is but one voice on the planet.

Musician and composer Paul Winter and the Paul Winter Consort created a Mass in celebration of Mother Earth and recorded it in the Cathedral of Saint John the Divine and the Grand Canyon. In addition to their musical instruments, they included the voices of the wolf, the whale, and the loon. The music is called *Missa Gaia/Earth Mass,* and it is dedicated to Saint Francis of Assisi on the year of his eight-hundredth birthday.

If you can, check out the music from the library. Choose a time when you are least likely to be interrupted. Take the phone off the hook. Sit or recline silently. Listen to the other voices. If you cannot find this recording, just sit quietly and listen.

Respond

God of human silence, at times I have valued human sound more than the voices of the rest of creation. I am eager to make their acquaintance. Give me the grace to be an attentive listener, to learn to identify each one by the sound of its voice, and to begin to understand the story each one has to tell.

Desert

Listen

Seeing the huge two hundred year old Saguaro cactus standing as sentinel over this desert life is moving beyond words. Touching a pink flowering caterpillar cactus, absorbing the green of a Paloverde bark, stepping on the sandy sea bed soil, climbing to an ancient cave overlooking an arroyo canyon literally stops you in your tracks. And then you can be even more attentive . . . to life, its textured variety of forms, and its interactive ecological systems.

As we begin to listen from a space of open reflection, it is likely that we will experience a grieving at what has been lost from our planet already and at what will disappear in our lifetime. As we acknowledge the sorrow or even the despair this entails we can begin to have a more realistic position from which to foster life and creative balance. This unacknowledged well of despair may prove to be a constructive source for action in spite of the apparent odds against achieving new modes of ecological equity and equilibrium in human-earth relations.

(Mary Evelyn Tucker)

◆ ◆ ◆ ◆ ◆

Reflect

A drive through the deserts of the Southwest, where the two-hundred-year-old Saguaro cacti stand, is a moving experience. These are cathedrals of the desert—awesome in stature, in their ability to survive the elements. There is also reason for grieving, as described by Mary Evelyn Tucker. People intentionally wound and kill these monuments to creation with rifles, shotguns, and other explosive devices. The survivors of heat and cold, drought and wind, rain and snow cannot defend themselves against human beings with their weapons of destruction.

Celie, in *The Color Purple*, says, "I knew that if I cut a tree, my arm would bleed." Reflect on how you can contribute in a concrete way to ecological equity and equilibrium in human-earth relations. Do you have some equivalent to the two-hundred-year-old Saguaro cacti in your locale for which you can be a protector?

Respond

My heart breaks, Creator God, at the senseless destruction of your creation. At times it seems that destructive forces outweigh constructive ones. Some days my spirit wanes. I find it difficult to notice images of hope. May this well of despair prove to be a constructive source for action.

Seaside

Listen

The shore is an ancient world, for as long as there has been an earth and sea there has been this place of the meeting of land and water. Yet it is a world that keeps alive the sense of continuing creation and of the relentless drive of life. Each time that I enter it, I gain some new awareness of its beauty and its deeper meanings, sensing that intricate fabric of life by which one creature is linked with another, and each with its surroundings.

(Rachel Carson)

◆ ◆ ◆ ◆ ◆

Reflect

Time magazine said of Rachel Carson's *The Edge of the Sea* that it catches "the life breath of science on the still glass of poetry." Science and poetry in partnership invite our mind and heart to begin to fathom the wonders of the seaside.

Sit in silence. Close your eyes. Imagine the seaside. Listen to the ebb and flow of the tide. Let yourself be carried by the rhythm of the waves to a place of inner peace.

Respond

God of all life-giving waters, how many times I return to the water's edge for solace and comfort. I am reminded of the safety of my mother's womb and the blessed gift of tears. I am grateful for all the ways the earth is moistened: rain, snow, dew, rivers, lakes, streams, oceans. May I be ever grateful for sacred water.

Bears of the Forest

Listen

We deprecate bears.

But grandly they blend with their native mountains. They roam the sandy slopes on lily meads, through polished glacier canyons, among the solemn firs and brown sequoia, manzanita, and chaparral, living upon red berries and gooseberries, little caring for rain or snow. . . . Magnificent bears of the Sierra are worthy of their magnificent homes. They are not companions of men, but children of God, and His charity is broad enough for bears. They are the objects of His tender keeping. . . .

Bears are made of the same dust as we, and breathe the same winds and drink of the same waters. A bear's days are warmed by the same sun, his dwellings are overdomed by the same blue sky, and his life turns and ebbs with heart-pulsings like ours, and was poured from the same First Fountain. And whether he at last goes to our stingy heaven or no, he has terrestrial immortality. His life not long, not short, knows no beginning, no ending. To him life unstinted, unplanned, is above the accidents of time, and his years, markless and boundless, equal Eternity.

God bless Yosemite bears!

(John Muir)

❖ ❖ ❖ ❖ ❖

Reflect

Naturalist John Muir is hailed as America's first environmental activist. His journals reveal a man whose time spent in the wilderness brought him to understand both the connections and the distinctions among all forms of life. His description of the place of the bear in creation's story shows a deep respect and love for these children of God.

Reflect on your understanding of the place of each of God's animal children in the ongoing creation story. How do you show them the respect and esteem that John Muir had for each of them? Can you think of any new ways that you can reverence and "bless" bears and other animals with whom we share the earth?

Respond

I am in awe of creatures great and small, O holy friend of bears. Help me to see these gentle giants with your eyes. Give me a heart that is large enough to include a grizzly bear and her cubs. May I learn to protect and defend their habitat so that they might flourish and give you praise.

Insects

Listen

Nine-tenths of all living creatures on the Earth are insects. They literally surround us. . . .

We are bombarded with messages that support the war against insects. . . .

Remembering how to rejoice in insects has to do with untangling the threads of misperceptions and fears that prevent us from including insects in our circle of community. . . .

At our center is a natural self at home in the world, a primitive, instinctual self which knows how to be in right relationship with insects. . . . How we translate this connection can determine how safe we feel in the world and how connected we feel to life.

(Joanne Hobbs Lauck)

◆ ◆ ◆ ◆ ◆

Reflect

No doubt we have all attended picnics where ants and flies have been uninvited guests. Summer hiking in the woods brings an onslaught of pesky mosquitos. At such times, rejoicing is rarely our first instinct. Nevertheless, with nine-tenths of all living creatures on the earth being insects, it stands to reason that they provide an important link in the cosmic chain.

In a society where bigger is often valued as better, that which is small can seem insignificant. Recall times when you have been aware of the presence of insects. Examine possible misperceptions and fears you might hold about insects. Begin to understand their connection to all other life in the creation story. Start, perhaps, with one type of insect—a bee is an easy choice—and ask yourself: Who depends on it? In what ways is it a marvel of creation? How does it serve us?

Respond

My attitudes and behaviors need to be transformed, O God. For too long I have ignored insects—except when they bother me. Increase my awareness. Help me to realize that insects share life with all God's creatures in a special way. Insects have much to teach me about patience, diligence, and resilience. May I be humble enough to learn from these, the least of my sisters and brothers.

Trees

Listen

I should like to
make my life's work
a gift of myself
to one tree.
Once I saw a tree
in Illinois.
Hypnotized by a
dull professor
into an altered
state, just
then I looked
out the window.
It was March
and the tree
was still
naked, magnificent.
I awakened too quickly
to remember its name,
but it had twelve arms
and thirteen elbows
and a bass oboe voice.
There are four trees
around my house.
Their invisible arms
reach out to protect
with a circle. I am
grateful and glad.
Meanwhile, though
I know their anthropoetic names:
crab, maple, red maple, silver birch,
it will take me forty years
to really see each tree

◆ ◆ ◆ ◆ ◆

and four hundred more to learn
the name each one calls itself.
By then we shall all
be changed anyway.
Schooled by the cardinal
and cedar waxwing
in the backyard
I have at least
figured this much out.

(Alla Renée Bozarth)

Reflect

A significant piece of the Garden story reveals humans naming all the other created beings. Nowhere in the story is the question, What do they call themselves?

Imagine. If other species could relate their story through human means of communication, what would they tell you? When you see a tree, a bird, a squirrel, consider their side of the creation story. God gifted us with imagination, in part so we could be empathetic—that is, put ourselves into someone else's shoes. Imagine what life is like for a tree in your neighborhood. How would the trees critique your care of the earth?

Respond

God who loves forests, something inside me goes numb when I consider the statistics: one acre of rainforest vanishes every second. Help me to feel both the beauty of a grove of trees and the anguish as those groves are being diminished. Today I will befriend a single tree and claim as my life's work to learn its name.

Gardening

Listen

One of my very favorite films anytime of the year is *Out of Africa*. I love the depiction of the art of storytelling in the film and the very haunting reflection of the storyteller—"I had a farm in Africa."

When I am old (older!) I will say, "I had a garden in Shoreview." For those of you who have been avid gardeners for years, you will smile at my novice enthusiasm. For the first time in my life, I had my own garden this past summer. The garden changed my heart. I planted, I weeded, I waited, I watched, I weeded, I harvested. When I was a child, I weeded in my mom's garden, but it wasn't the same. I had to be older and a little life-weather-beaten to understand the spirituality of dirt. The farmers and gardeners among you will understand. There is a sacred connection with the Creator of the firmament that only happens when your hands are "digging in the dirt." Now I know why people page through seed catalogues in January when the earth is anything but giving. There is a sweet anticipation to connect with Mother Earth.

(Colleen Conlin Vlaisavljevich)

Reflect

In early spring all types of gardening gloves show up in the stores. Gardeners spend time choosing just the right pair, resolving to wear them this year. Generally, the gloves come along on the first outing for blister prevention during leaf raking, soil turning, and removing last year's leftover root clumps. When the time comes for planting, off come the gloves—"there is a sweet anticipation to connect with Mother Earth." Touching the seeds, the plants, the soil, we become firmly grounded and rooted in our patch of the larger garden. The sacred connection occurs. Home again, at last. The gloves? Next year for sure!

Care of the earth begins where you are, in whatever ways you can. Experience the sacred connection with the Creator of the firmament. Care for a houseplant, start a window herb garden, join a community gardening committee. Give your hands the gift of digging in the earth—gloves optional!

Respond

My earthy God, I feel closest to you when I give myself over to the garden. I feel a sense of caring and concern, focus and friendship. May my days in the garden be a love affair with the soil and with the millions of creatures who live in the garden. And may I always be mindful that you are the Gardener who gently tends us all.

Summer

Listen

Sun and sky mirrored the green of the spinach.
In the tin pail shaded by yellow paper
Well-water kept cool at the start of the rows.
The water had an iron taste, and the air,
Even, a tang of metal.
                    Day in, day out,
I bent over the plants in my leather-kneed
Dungarees, proud as a lady in a sea
Of prize roses, culling the fullest florets;
My world pyramided with laden baskets.
I'd only to set one foot in wilderness—
A whole sea of spinach-heads leaned to my hand.

                                          (Sylvia Plath)

◆ ◆ ◆ ◆ ◆

Reflect

Few things are as tender as being welcomed home after time away. Perhaps it is the recognition of a family member at a holiday reunion. Perhaps it is the companion animal who meets us at the front door after a day of work. Or, perhaps, it is just the summer vegetables who greet us when we go to harvest. Sylvia Plath describes such a scene of friendly recognition and self-gift. The spinach plants have been so well tended that they willingly bend toward the hand of their caregiver—a fitting description of the ripeness of summer.

Set aside time to look through a summertime photo album. Notice how many pictures are taken out in nature. Be aware of how many pictures are taken with family. Allow yourself to understand that nature is not a backdrop for family events but it is your extended family. Allow yourself to imagine that nature waits for you to come outside during summer, like a family member waits for your return home.

Respond

God of the ever changing seasons, may I be filled with a deep gratitude and appreciation for the way I am nurtured in summer. May I take time to celebrate my time outdoors.

Autumn

Listen

The morns are meeker than they were,
The nuts are getting brown;
The berry's cheek is plumper,
The rose is out of town.
The maple wears a gayer scarf,
The field a scarlet gown.
Lest I should be old-fashioned,
I'll put a trinket on.

(Emily Dickinson)

◆ ◆ ◆ ◆ ◆

Reflect

The autumn equinox is a celebration of lengthening evenings. Nights get longer and cooler. Fruits ripen, flowers fade, and gardens are put to bed. The air feels almost bittersweet. Leaves fall in gratitude for the colors that they bear. It is a time of gathering, harvesting, settling in for the long wait ahead. But it is also, as Emily Dickinson suggests, a time for festivity. Autumn calls us to decorate our life with nature's bounty and to realize that what happens to nature also happens to our body.

Close your eyes, and imagine that you are on a long autumn walk. Breathe in deeply, and be aware of the aromas in the air. Notice the leaves and how they crunch when you walk on them. Imagine their color and texture. If it is autumn, take this mindful stroll.

Respond

God of all changes, sometimes I am afraid of what is happening to my aging body. Like an autumn landscape, I see my body moving from its ripeness to its harvest-time. Help me to see, with the poet's eye, that aging is one way to put on a new trinket. Let me see age as an adornment, and the autumn of my life and of all nature as another gift from you.

Circles

Listen

Everything the Power of the World does is done in a circle. The sky is round, and I have heard that the earth is round like a ball, and so are all the stars. The wind, in its greatest power, whirls. Birds make their nests in circles, for theirs is the same religion as ours. The sun comes forth and goes down again in a circle. The moon does the same, and both are round. Even the seasons form a great circle in their changing, and always come back again to where they were. The life of a man is a circle from childhood to childhood, and so it is in everything where power moves.

(Black Elk)

❖ ❖ ❖ ❖ ❖

Reflect

Life has a familiar rhythm that Black Elk describes as a circle. Wherever we go, we encounter this roundness: in the trunks of trees, in ripples in pools of water, and in the shape of new life in the womb.

Our actions oftentimes happen in circles. Most of us are probably familiar with the old saying, "What goes around, comes around." For the Hindu, this is called *karma*. For the Christian, this is called the Golden Rule: doing unto others what we would like done to us. The earth teaches us that all life has consequences that come back to us, for everything is connected in a great circle of life.

Go outside, and consider all the circles that you see in nature. Then sit quietly, and ask yourself how your actions are coming back to you, how the good and the destructive come back to you. Offer a prayer of gratitude for the power of circles.

Respond

God who moves in circles, I have often thought that the shortest distance between two points is a straight line. Today I see that circles and roundness are your gifts. Let me learn from nature how life is seasonal and rhythmic. Grant me grateful awareness of how my actions come back to me and affect others in this great circle of life.

Darkness

Listen

The sun does not penetrate all of space. Much of space is dark. Much of the birth of the cosmos itself was done in the dark—the sun has not always existed. The seed under ground is growing in the dark no less than the fetus in the mother's womb. All mystery is about the dark. All darkness is about mystery.
(Matthew Fox)

The imagery that depicts only light as holy and darkness as evil has dualistic roots. It fails to recognize that both the dark and the light can be blessing places and that either too much dark or too much light can be a curse. When we are gentle with our own darkness, compassion grows for the foibles and shadows of others rather than self-righteous condemnation.
(William Fitzgerald)

◆ ◆ ◆ ◆ ◆

Reflect

Quietly reflect on the light and the dark in your life. How can the dark moments be seen as times of hibernation and resting? How can the light moments be seen as times of energy and action? Examine the ways you need both rest and action, both dark and light. Offer the following prayer in celebration of darkness. Take time with the prayer, letting its wisdom settle in your soul.

Respond

O God, Black is Beautiful!
Let us be aware of black blessings:
Blessed be the black night that nurtures dreams,
Blessed be the black cave of imagination that births
      creativity,
Blessed be dark wombs that cradle us,
Blessed be black loam that feeds our bodies.
. . . .
Blessed be black energy that swirls into gracefulness,
Blessed be black coal that heats us,
Blessed be black boiling clouds hurling down lightning
      and cleansing rain,
Blessed be even our own darkness, our raw, undeveloped
      cave of shadows.
O God, when we befriend black and do not deny its
      power,
Black is beautiful indeed!
May we discover blessings
within our holy dark!

(William Fitzgerald)

Eating

Listen

Eating, more than any other human activity, binds us to the world of nature. It is the vital bridge that connects human culture with the larger environment. The kinds of plants and animals that a society chooses to expropriate and consume provide a mirror to the values and relationships of that society. That is why, in most cultures, eating is celebrated as a sacred act, as well as an act of survival and replenishment. . . .

Restoring biodiversity on the earth and restructuring the agricultural practices and eating habits of Americans . . . require not only a change in our personal dietary choices but also a change in our relationship to the natural world from which we draw our sustenance.

. . . A change in eating habits must also be accompanied by a personal transformation grounded in a new appreciation of the sacred value of the biological community of which we are a part.

By championing genetic diversity and making a personal choice to change our eating habits to reflect our concern for the larger biological community, we help prepare the ground for a new age in history—one in which we accept our responsibility to be caretakers of the earth.

(Jeremy Rifkin)

◆ ◆ ◆ ◆ ◆

Reflect

Twenty-five years ago, world-renowned chef and environmentalist Alice Waters opened *Chez Panisse* restaurant in Oakland, California. The unique character of the restaurant was its serving of only the foods that were in season in the immediate bioregion. When speaking of food, Alice Waters refers to the relational aspects: the diner's relationship to the food, to the region, and to those who are sharing the meal. She frequently advises guests, "Choose something from the menu that all of you can share"—a prophetic example of the appreciation of the sacred value of the biological community of which we are a part.

Review your eating habits. Do you know why you eat what you eat? Are you aware of where and how the food you eat is grown? Take one food you commonly eat: ponder its source, how it is brought to you, how it is handled, and the nourishment it provides. Give thanks for it.

Respond

God who gives us bread for the journey, help me to see each meal as a eucharist. May I be aware of the community of life that conspires to nourish me every day. I pray for the grace to be truly grateful and to have my table open to all.

Food

Listen

It has become clear to me that the concept of food itself is key to the transformation of our ecological crisis. Unless our human species can open itself to the contemplation of food as a holy mystery through which we *eat ourselves into existence,* then the meaning of existence will continue to elude us. Our present cultural experience of food has degenerated into food as *fuel,* supplying energy for our insatiable search to fill the soul's hungers. When we understand that food is not a metaphor for spiritual nourishment, but is itself spiritual, then we eat food with a spiritual attitude and taste and are nourished by the Divine *directly.* . . .

If we were to accept the earth on the terms and under the exquisite conditions in which it continues to evolve, the role of the farmer would be raised to a most honorable and sacred human profession. . . . Farmers might understand themselves as acting in something akin to a prophetic and priestly role. We need to see farmers as entering the sanctuary of the soil and engaging the mysterious forces of creation in order to bless and nourish the inner and outer life of the community they serve.

(Miriam Therese MacGillis)

◆ ◆ ◆ ◆ ◆

Reflect

The giving-way of the family farm to corporate agriculture industry signals a tragic, possibly irretrievable loss of the relational character of humans with the land and the growing process. The farm was related to the family, as was the family to the farm—generation after generation. Something inside us understands the importance of that relationship, as evidenced by the thousands of folks who make weekly pilgrimage to local co-ops or farmers' markets. They honor the relationship of the grower to the food, and of the food to their own body. It is a profound image of hope for blessing and nourishing the inner and outer life of the community.

Meditate on the spiritual nature of food. Make a trip to your local co-op or farmers' market. Bring home some garden-fresh vegetables. Prepare, bless, and share this sacred feast with your friends and family.

Respond

God of the harvest, blessed be the hands that plant. Blessed be the hands that harvest. Blessed be the hands that prepare. Blessed be those who are nourished to do your work in the world.

The Spirit of All Things

Listen

The Holy Spirit is life that gives life,
Moving all things.
It is the root in every creature
And purifies all things,
Wiping away sins,
Anointing wounds.
It is radiant life, worthy of praise,
Awakening and enlivening
All things.

(Hildegard of Bingen)

Reflect

Hildegard of Bingen lived in tumultuous times. Radical changes—necessary changes—were occurring on a daily basis. As abbess of a huge monastery, she found herself embroiled in most of them. At the heart of her prophetic courage was her understanding that the ultimate source of all good change is the Holy Spirit. Her faith in the presence of the Holy Spirit in all things supported her unwavering fidelity to the transformation of her world.

Whenever you feel alone, grow weary, or lose heart in the struggle for care of the earth, recall the faith of Hildegard. Pray to the Holy Spirit.

Respond

Sometimes, God, I feel as though I need new energy in my soul. I grow bone-weary with commitments, obligations, and responsibilities. Help me remember that your Spirit has been poured out on all creation to heal, anoint, awaken, and enliven. Give me the steady, pulsing energy I so desperately need.

Time

Listen

In order to gain any insight into the meaning of life in the 1990's from an ecological, Christian perspective, we must understand ourselves within the largest historical context. If we imagine that our 15 billion year history was compressed into a single calendar year . . . the Milky Way galaxy self-organized in late February, our solar system emerged from the elemental stardust of an exploded supernova in early September, the planetary oceans formed in mid-September, Earth awakened into life in late September, sex was invented in late November, the dinosaurs lived for a few days in early December, Flowering plants burst upon the scene with a dazzling array of color in mid-December, and the universe began reflecting consciously in and through the human, with choice and free will, less than ten minutes before midnight on December 31!

Earth has not been thinking reflexively for long at all. We have only known that we were Earth thinking about itself for the last few seconds.

(Michael Dowd)

◆ ◆ ◆ ◆ ◆

Reflect

We are the heirs to an unfathomably long history! As humans, we sometimes imagine ourselves as the crown of creation. Yet, a universal calendar—all of time compressed into one year—shows us that we are only minutes old. Having humanity dictating earth's evolutionary future is like having the newborn take care of the family's checkbook. We are simply too new on the scene to be overly smug. But we can use our power of thought to reflect on our actions and to learn to honor our ancestors in creation.

Imagine that you were present at the initial flaring forth of the Creator's Big Bang. Watch each stage of creation as it is briefly described in the calendar. How does it feel? What do you notice when each creative event happens?

Respond

God of all history, give me a healthy awareness of time. Let me know that my actions today will affect generations to come. Help me to be grateful for the stages of creation. May I be aware that you called forth each of them in love.

Solitary Existence

Listen

And to speak of solitude again, it becomes always clearer that this is at bottom not something that one can take or leave. We *are* solitary. We may delude ourselves and act as though this were not so. That is all. But how much better it is to realize that we are so, yes, even to begin by assuming it. We shall indeed turn dizzy then; for all points upon which our eye has been accustomed to rest are taken from us, there is nothing near any more and everything far is infinitely far. . . . So for him who becomes solitary all distances, all measures change; of these changes many take place suddenly, and then, as with the man on the mountaintop, extraordinary imaginings and singular sensations arise that seem to grow out beyond all bearing. But it is necessary for us to experience *that* too. We must assume our existence as *broadly* as we in any way can; everything, even the unheard-of, must be possible in it.

(Rainer Maria Rilke)

◆ ◆ ◆ ◆ ◆

Reflect

Creation, while so much a community, is also solitary. There is a starkness to the reality that each creature is unique, unrepeatable, and solitary. Each creature is different, and it stands alone in that difference. But each creature is not isolated. Rilke affirms that awareness of our solitariness can be dizzying. It can be overwhelming and terrifying. Or, it can be a stepping-off point to celebrate our difference—a way to celebrate possibilities.

Pause for a moment and consider what makes you different and special. Be specific. Consider specific gifts you bring to the world. Reflect on how these same gifts also, at times, separate you from others. Consider how the very thing that makes you special can also make you solitary.

Respond

God who creates diversity, help me to appreciate the differences I see in myself and other creatures. Sometimes I am so numb from feeling alone and solitary that I find it hard to appreciate that which makes me different. Help me to know that even feeling solitary is a celebration of your creation.

Connection

Listen

This we know. . . . All things are connected like the blood which unites one family. All things are connected.

Whatever befalls the earth befalls the sons of the earth. Man does not weave the web of life, he is merely a strand in it. Whatever he does to the web, he does to himself.

. . . When the last red man has vanished from this earth, and his memory is only the shadow of a cloud moving across the prairie, those shores and forests will still hold the spirits of my people. For they love this earth as the new-born loves its mother's heartbeat. So if we sell you our land, love it as we've loved it. Care for it as we've cared for it. Hold in your mind the memory of the land as it is when you take it. And with all your strength, with all your mind, with all your heart, preserve it for your children and love it . . . as God loves us all.

One thing we know. Our God is the same God. . . . Even the white man cannot be exempt from the common destiny. We may be brothers after all. We shall see.

(Chief Seattle)

Reflect

The white children of God have undoubtedly strayed from the understanding of the Native American man and woman regarding the interconnectedness of all created things and the importance of respecting them in their own right. Chief Seattle was prophetic. Whatever we do to the web of life, we do to ourselves. Already we are living with the devastating effects of nuclear testing, toxic waste, industrial pollution, deforestation, and countless other consequences of shortsighted actions and of being disconnected from the earth. With all that has been needlessly destroyed, and all that is in the process of destruction, what will be left for the children?

Close your eyes, and call to mind an outdoor place you held precious in your youth. Remember the times you escaped to that place. How did it feel? What did you do there? How does that place look now?

Respond

God of the land, the native people of the Americas offer the gift of connection. May I be made aware of the consequences of my actions and choices on future generations. May I grow in understanding that every creature is my relative. Immersed in newfound connections, may I work to secure a future of hope for all who depend on Mother Earth.

Cosmic Dance

Listen

The Lord plays and diverts Himself in the garden of His creation, and if we could let go of our own obsession with what we think is the meaning of it all, we might be able to hear His call and follow Him in His mysterious, cosmic dance. We do not have to go very far to catch echoes of that game, and of that dancing. When we are alone on a starlit night; when by chance we see the migrating birds in autumn descending on a grove of junipers to rest and eat; when we see children in a moment when they are really children; when we know love in our own hearts; or when, like the Japanese poet Basho we hear an old frog land in a quiet pond with a solitary splash—at such times the awakening, the turning inside out of all values, the "newness," the emptiness and the purity of vision that make themselves evident, provide a glimpse of the cosmic dance. . . . The fact remains that we are invited to forget ourselves on purpose, cast our awful solemnity to the winds and join in the general dance.

(Thomas Merton)

♦ ♦ ♦ ♦ ♦

Reflect

We have been escorted to a grand and lovely cosmic dance. Set in motion some fifteen billion years ago, we are the most recent guests to accept the Creator's invitation to join in a rhythmic celebration of life.

Part of learning to dance is learning to appreciate the music and the dance space. In spiritual terms, it is learning to contemplate, to see sacred space. This universe, in all its diversity, complexity, history, and beauty, is really one sacred space in which God is constantly glorified through the dance and song of all creatures.

Sit outside for thirty minutes. Give yourself time to observe. Resist having an agenda for the time; simply notice. Reread the passage by Merton, and add to his description of natural occurrences that are "echoes of that game, and of that dancing." Of course, if you feel like dancing, do so.

Respond

For the rhythm of life, O God of the dance, I am grateful. For the opportunity to participate, I am humbled. For the possibilities of life, I am open and willing—your partner in the cosmic dance. Amen. Alleluia.

Acknowledgments *(continued)*

The psalms in this book are from *Psalms Anew: In Inclusive Language,* compiled by Nancy Schreck and Maureen Leach (Winona, MN: Saint Mary's Press, 1986). Copyright © 1986 by Saint Mary's Press. All rights reserved.

All other scriptural quotations in this book are from the New Revised Standard Version of the Bible. Copyright © 1989 by the Division of Christian Education of the National Council of the Churches of Christ in the United States of America. All rights reserved.

The excerpt on page 8 by Bayazid is quoted from *The Song of the Bird,* by Anthony de Mello (New York: Image Books, 1982), page 153. Copyright © 1982 by Anthony de Mello, SJ.

The excerpt on page 11 by Vincent de Paul is from *La Vie du Venerable Serviteur de Dieu Vincent de Paul,* by Louis Abelly (Paris: Florentin Lambert, 1664), pages 177–178.

The excerpt on page 12 by Teresa of Ávila is from *The Book of Her Life,* in *The Collected Works of St. Teresa of Ávila,* translated by Kieran Kavanaugh and Otilio Rodriguez (Washington, DC: ICS Publications, 1976), page 137.

The excerpt on page 14 is from *The Awakened Heart,* by Gerald May (New York: HarperCollins Publishers, 1991), page 110. Copyright © 1991 by Gerald May.

The excerpts on pages 19, 36, and 48 are from *The Body of God: An Ecological Theology,* by Sallie McFague (Minneapolis: Fortress Press, 1993), pages 19, 122–123, and 211, respectively. Copyright © 1993 by Augsburg Fortress.

The poem, "Pax," on page 21 is from *The Complete Poems of D. H. Lawrence,* vol. 2, collected and edited by Vivian de Sola Pinto and F.W. Roberts (New York: Viking Press, 1964), page 700. Copyright © 1964, 1971 by Angelo Ravagli and C. M. Weekley, executors of the estate of Frieda Lawrence Ravagli. Used by permission of Viking Penguin, a division of Penguin Putnam, New York and Laurence Pollinger Limited, London.

The excerpts on page 22 are from *The Simone Weil Reader,* edited by George A. Panichas (New York: David McKay Company, 1977), pages 472 and 474. Copyright © 1977 by George A. Panichas.

The excerpt on pages 24–25 is from *Befriending the Earth: A Theology of Reconciliation Between the Humans and the Earth,* by Thomas Berry, CP, in dialogue with Thomas Clarke, SJ, edited by Stephen Dunn, CP, and Anne Lonergan (Mystic, CT: Twenty-Third Publications, 1991), page 9. Copyright © 1991 by Holy Cross Centre of Ecology and Spirituality.

The excerpts on pages 28 and 50 are from *The Universe Story: From the Primordial Flaring Forth to the Ecozoic Era—A Celebration of the Unfolding of the Cosmos,* by Brian Swimme and Thomas Berry (San Francisco: HarperSanFrancisco, 1992), pages 268 and 44–45. Copyright © 1992 by Brian Swimme. Reprinted by permission of HarperCollins Publishers.

The excerpt on page 30 is from "Retrieval of the Cosmos in Theology," by Elizabeth Johnson, in *EarthLight,* spring 1997, pages 8–9. Copyright © 1997 by Unity with Nature Committee.

The excerpt on page 32 is from *Jesus and the Cosmos,* by Denis Edwards (Mahwah, NJ: Paulist Press, 1991), page 24. Copyright © 1991 by Denis Edwards.

The excerpts on pages 38 and 57 are from *The Color Purple,* by Alice Walker (New York: Washington Square Press, Pocket Books, 1982), page 178. Copyright © 1982 by Alice Walker.

The excerpt on page 40 is from *The Music of Silence: Entering the Sacred Space of Monastic Experience,* by David Steindl-Rast, OSB, with Sharon Lebell (San Francisco: HarperSanFrancisco, n.d.), pages 35–36.

The excerpt on page 42 is from *Ecology and Liberation: A New Paradigm,* by Leonardo Boff, translated by John Cumming (Maryknoll, NY: Orbis Books, 1995), page 7. English translation copyright © 1995 by Orbis Books.

The excerpt on page 46 is from *The Best of Meister Eckhart,* edited by Halcyon Backhouse (New York: Crossroad Publishing, 1992), page 138. Copyright © 1992 by Halcyon Backhouse.

The excerpt on page 52 is from *Journal of a Solitude,* by May Sarton (New York: W. W. Norton and Company, 1973), page 16–17. Copyright © 1973 by May Sarton.

The excerpt on page 54 is from *Dakota: A Spiritual Geography,* by Kathleen Norris (New York: Houghton Mifflin Company, 1993), page 10. Copyright © 1993 by Kathleen Norris.

The excerpt on page 56 is from "Earth Literacy for Theology," by Mary Evelyn Tucker, in *EarthLight,* summer 1996, page 6. Copyright © 1996 by Unity with Nature Committee.

The excerpt on page 58 is from *The Edge of the Sea,* by Rachel Carson (Boston: Houghton Mifflin Company, 1979), page 2. Copyright © 1955 by Rachel L. Carson.

The excerpt on page 60 is from *Baptized into Wilderness: A Christian Perspective on John Muir,* by Richard Cartwright Austin (Abingdon, VA: Creekside Press, 1991), page 58. Copyright © 1991 by Richard Cartwright Austin.

The excerpt on page 62 is from "Redrawing the Circle: A New Relationship with Insects," by Joanne Hobbs Lauck, in *EarthLight,* fall 1997, pages 8–9. Copyright © 1997 by Unity with Nature Committee.

The poem on pages 64–65 is from *Stars in Your Bones: Emerging Signposts on Our Spiritual Journeys,* by Alla Renée Bozarth, Julia Barkley, and Terri Berthiaume Hawthorne (Saint Cloud, MN: North Star Press of Saint Cloud, 1990), page 71. Copyright © 1990 by Alla Renée Bozarth, Julia Barkley, and Terri Berthiaume Hawthorne. Permission applied for.

The excerpt on page 66 is taken from a Christmas letter written by Colleen Conlin Vlaisavljevich. Used with permission.

Excerpts from the poem "Memoirs of a Spinach-Picker" on page 68 are from *The Collected Poems: Sylvia Plath,* edited by Ted Hughes (New York: Harper and Row, Publishers, 1981), pages 89–90. Copyright © 1959 by the Estate of Sylvia Plath. Reprinted by permission of HarperCollins Publishers.

The poem on page 70 is from *The Collected Poems of Emily Dickinson* (New York: Barnes and Noble Books, 1993), page 124. Copyright © 1993 by Barnes and Noble Books.

The excerpt on page 72 is from *Black Elk Speaks: Being the Life Story of a Holy Man of the Oglala Sioux,* as told through John G. Neihardt (Flaming Rainbow) (Lincoln, NE: University of Nebraska Press, 1961), pages 198–199. Copyright © 1961 by the University of Nebraska Press.

The first excerpt by Matthew Fox on page 74 is from *Original Blessing: A Primer in Creation Spirituality Presented in Four Paths, Twenty-Six Themes, and Two Questions,* by Matthew Fox (Santa Fe, NM: Bear and Company, 1983), page 136. Copyright © 1983 by Bear and Company.

The second excerpt on page 74 and the poem on page 75 by William Fitzgerald are taken from *Praying,* November–December 1997, page 15. Copyright © 1997 by the National Catholic Reporter Publishing Company. Used by permission.

The excerpts on pages 76 and 78 are from "Reclaiming Eating as Sacred Relationship," by Jeremy Rifkin, and "Feeding the Soul from the Sacred Earth," by Miriam Therese MacGillis, in *EarthLight*, fall 1996, pages 5 and 9. Copyright © 1996 by Unity with Nature Committee.

The poem on page 80 is from *Hildegard of Bingen: Mystical Writings*, edited by Fiona Bowie and Oliver Davies (New York: Crossroad Publishing, 1990), page 118. Copyright © 1990 by Fiona Bowie and Oliver Davies. Permission applied for.

The excerpt on page 82 is from *Earthspirit: A Handbook for Nurturing an Ecological Christianity*, by Michael Dowd (Mystic, CT: Twenty-Third Publications, 1991), page 23. Copyright © 1991 by Michael Dowd.

The excerpt on page 84 is from *Letters to a Young Poet*, by Rainer Maria Rilke (New York: W. W. Norton and Company, 1954), pages 66–67. Revised edition copyright © 1954 by W. W. Norton and Company.

The excerpt on page 86 by Chief Seattle is from *Thinking Like a Mountain: Towards a Council of All Beings*, by John Seed, Joanna Macy, Pat Fleming, and Arnie Naess (Philadelphia: New Society Publishers, 1988), pages 71–73. Copyright © 1988 by John Seed.

The excerpt on page 88 is from *Thomas Merton: Spiritual Master*, edited by Lawrence S. Cunningham (Mahwah, NJ: Paulist Press, 1992), page 256. Copyright © 1992 by Lawrence S. Cunningham.

Titles in the Life in Abundance series

Growing in Care of the Earth
by Virginia Pharr and Janet Watson

Growing in Courage by Peter Gilmour

Growing in Hope by Lou Anne M. Tighe

Growing in Joy by Robert F. Morneau

Order from your local bookstore or from
Saint Mary's Press
702 Terrace Heights
Winona, MN 55987-1320
USA
1-800-533-8095

Jesus said, . . . "I came that [you] may have life, and have it abundantly" (John 10:7–10).

Jesus' mission is accomplished in each one of us when we nourish the seeds of full life that God has planted in the garden of our soul.